KNOW AN AMPLIFIER WHEN IT IS PARAMETRIC

GOPAL CHAKRABORTY | SUBHASIS SAHA | NIRATYAY BISWAS

Dedicated

to

the memory of my beloved Father

Late Sankar Chakraborty

(Father of Gopal Chakraborty)

My beloved Father

Subhash Chandra Saha

(Father of Subhasis Saha)

and My beloved Mother

Sourabhi Biswas

(Mother of Niratyay Biswas)

Their honesty and devotion to education is ever rememberable

Contents

FOREWORD

This book is written on the topic Parametric Amplifier. The parametric amplifier uses a device whose reactance is varied in such a manner that amplification results. Fundamental properties of electronics parametric amplifier is described here with model and mathematical analysis. This book helps you to understand the basics of electronics parametric amplifier.

PREFACE

This book on "Know an Amplifier when it is Parametric" has been written with a view to understand the basics of Parametric Amplifier specially in electronic device. This newly edition of book is written in accordance with the new syllabus introduced by MAKAUT for the higher semester students of both Electonics and Communication Engineering department and Electrical Engineering department. This book have been done for the benefits of students, We hope this edition will also be well accepted by my respected teachers and my beloved students.

The book has been written in very lucid and simple English. While presenting the subject matter, it has been my constant conscious effort to give more depth of treatment and emphasis on the fundamentals.

I hope, this publication will also be response equally well by respected teachers and my beloved students like previous editions of this book. Any suggestions, comments and constructive criticism of this first edition of this book are cordially invited and thank fully acknowledged both from students and teachers for further improvement of this book.

I

CHAPTER 1: RIVEW OF INSTABILITY

CHAPTER 1: RIVEW OF INSTABILITY

1.1 Motivation

Curiosity is one of the most vital words in science. It is one of the most important key to unfold the mysteries. To solve this curiosity we need to do experiment, record and analyze the results. In our case we are doing practical realization of parametric instability with the help of electronic circuit (parametric amplifier) and mechanical length varying pendulum. Michael Faraday (1831) first to notice the oscillation of one frequency being excited by forces of double the frequency in the crispation observes in a wine glass excited to "sing". Melde(1859) generated parametric oscillations in a sting by employing a tuning fork to periodically vary the tension at twice the resonance frequency of a string. Parametric oscillation was first treated as a general phenomenon by Rayleigh. Parametric amplifier was first use in 1913.Parametric Oscillator is used in many applications. It has been developed as low noise amplifier especially in the radio and microwave frequency range which has many communicating applications. Another common use of parametric amplifier or low noise amplifier is frequency conversion, as for example conversion from audio to radio frequency. It has application in biological system, which can be readily used in medical science. Mechanical parametric pendulum is used to measure the intensity of earthquake. we see that parametric instability has so many applications which can motivated anyone to work with it in this area of study.

1.2 Introduction

A system is unstable when it exhibits limit cycle behavior. After being excited if the system does not come back in its stable state, the system becomes unstable.

Instability in system is generally characterized by some of the output or internal states growing without bounds not all system that is not stable is unstable. System can also be marginally stable or exhibits limit cycle behavior.

The system is unstable if any of the root of its characteristic equation has real part greater then zero. This is equivalent to any of the eigen value of state matrix having real part greater than zero.

Here in the figure: 1.1 the position of the ball at the top of a hill shape object is an example of instability. The position of the ball is not stable; it may fell down either side of the object at any moment at any time.

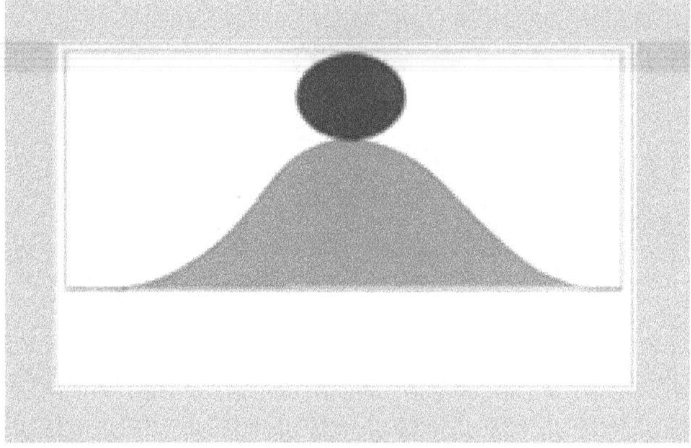

Fig 1.1: Unstable System

The solution of the differential equation of a network function is given as-

$$i(t) = k e^{S_n t} = k e^{\sigma_n t + j\omega_n t}$$

(1.1)

Where S_n is the complex root of the characteristic equation given as-

$$S_n = \sigma_n + j\omega_n$$

(1.2)

Where first part of equation 1.2 is the real part and the second one is imaginary part. Now when the real part of equation 1.2 is greater than zero the system become unstable.

1.3 What is parametric instability?

If any property of a system varying nonlinearly for changing the parameter of system by a negligible value then the property of that system is called parametric instability.

Name of the different physical system where parametric instability is found:
1. Electronic system (as for example, parametric amplifier)
2. Mechanical system (as for example, three coupled oscillator, parametric pendulum)
3. Optical system (OPA)
4. Biological system (Parkinsons's disease) etc.

1.4 Amplifier:

An amplifier is a device wherein an "agent" is driven by a local source of power, has motion imparted to it and hence gains energy of motion. This "agent" then by geometry or circuitry has its movement affected, and energy released in an external circuit by the expenditure of less energy in the input or controlling element. This is essentially a classical description of an amplifier. It will be most strained when used to describe the quantum mechanical amplifiers where energy of motion is imparted to the spin of a bound electron in a paramagnetic ion and the geometry or circuitry is relatively hidden emission process. In a vacuum tube amplifier the "agent" is, of course, a free electron. The motion imparted to it is translational motion. Its kinetic energy is derived from the local source of power, i.e., the voltage across the anode to cathode spacing and the current in the anode circuit. The controlling element is the control grid which by geometry is capable of changing the kinetic energy of the electrons by a greater amount than the energy it consumes itself in the process.

While the local sources of power fall into two classes, direct power and alternating power, the agents employed are many and varied. The proper choice of power source depends on the agent employed.

First, if the movement of this agent is free and unidirectional, the source of power can be direct. Examples are the free electron in the vacuum tube, the translational motion of electrons or holes in the semiconductor transistor amplifier and Esaki diode amplifier.

Second, if the movement of this agent is bound or constrained at some limit the source of power must alternate. An example is the use of domain walls as the agent in a magnetic amplifier where the wall motion is constrained by the dimensions of the material or by complete alignment with the field.

Other examples are the charge on the capacitance of a P-N junction (the Varactor parametric amplifier), or the quantized spin orientations of the Maser. All of these agents, since they are bound or constrained, require alternating power to excite them. Chart I shows a classification of amplifiers as to direct local power and alternating local power. The nature of the amplifying "agent" and the approximate operating frequency range is indicated in each case. In this study we will confine ourselves to the alternating local power type of amplifier and call these collectively parametric amplifiers.

II
CHAPTER 2: PARAMETRIC AMPLIFIER

2.1 Introduction

A parametric amplifier is named because of its operation due to the periodic variation of the device's parameters such as capacitance of a varactor diode. Under the influence of a suitable pump signal the output of the amplifier increases non-linearly.

It is a highly sensitive low noise amplifier for ultra high frequency and microwave radio signals, utilizing as the active element an inductor or capacitor whose reactance is varied periodically at another microwave or ultra high frequency. Amplification of weak signal waves occur through a nonlinear modulation or signal mixing process which produces additional signal wave at other frequency. This process may provide negative resistance amplification for the applied signal wave and increased power in one or more of the new frequency which are generated. There are different type of parametric amplifier circuit, such as parametric up-converter, negative resistance amplifier e.t.c.

The term "varactor" comes from the English expression for *variable reactor* and indicates semiconductor diodes, which utilize the dependence of the diode capacitance on the operating point of the diode. It is a type of diode which has a variable capacitance that is a function of the voltage impressed on its terminals. It is principally used as a voltage-controlled capacitor, and its diode function is secondary. It is operated reverse-biased so no current flows through it, but since the width of the depletion region varies with the applied bias voltage, the capacitance of the diode can be made to vary. The circuit symbol and the cross-section of a Varactor diode are shown in figures 2.1 & 2.2. The equivalent circuit diagram of varactor diode is shown in figure 2.3

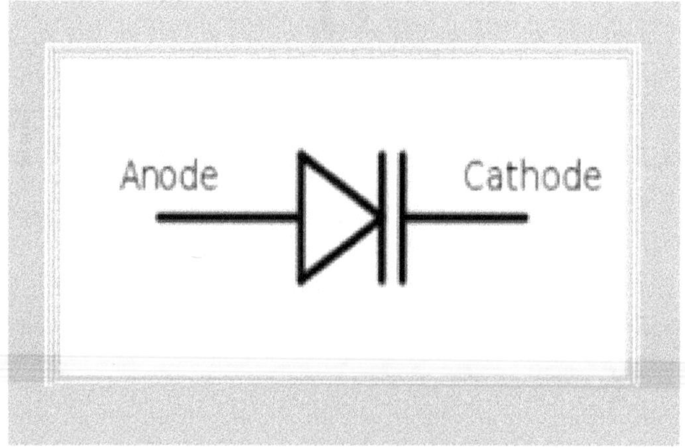

Fig 2.1: Schematic symbol Varactor diode

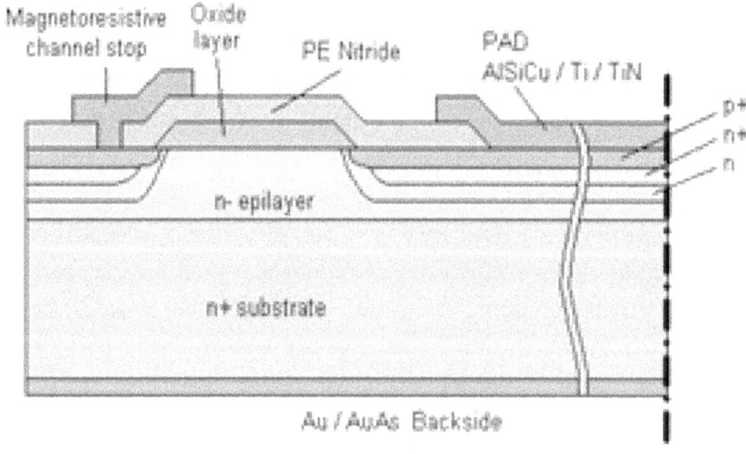

Fig 2.2: The cross-section of Varactor diode

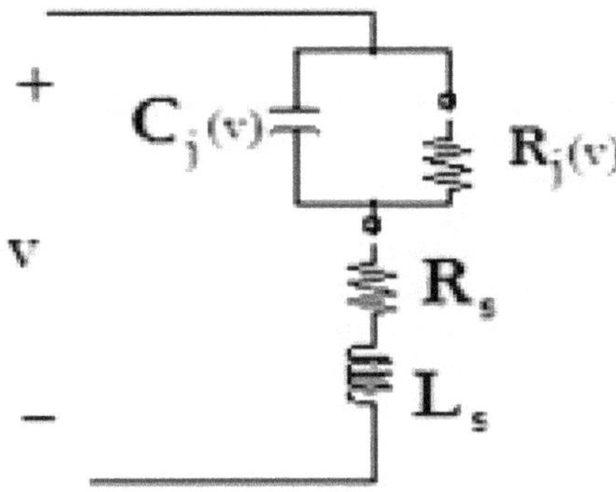

Fig 2.3: Varactor equivalent circuit

Under the influence of a suitable pump signal. If a small input signal at a frequency f_s and the ac power source operated as a pumping signal at a frequency f_p, are applied together to the varactor diode, linear amplification of a small signal results in due to time-varying capacitance of the diode. Pump signal provides the power required for amplification and the power output is either at the input frequency f_s or at the idler frequency $f_i = f_p - f_s$.

The circuit diagram of a basic parametric amplifier is shown in the figure 2.4

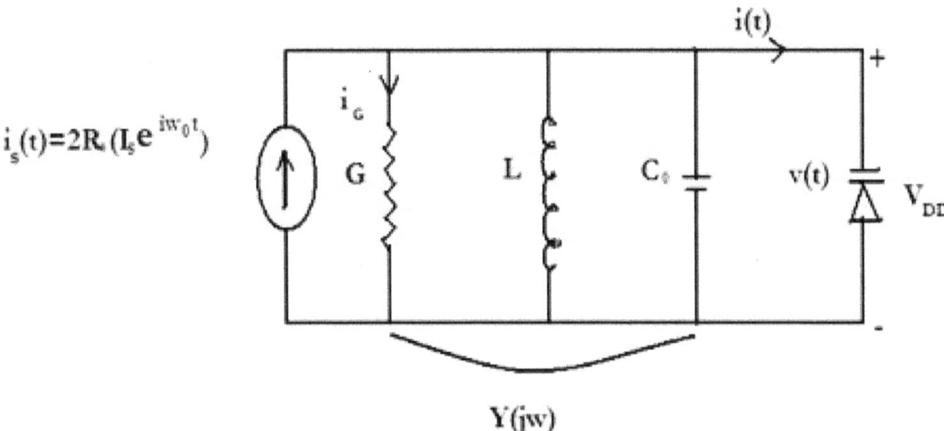

Fig 2.4 Circuit diagram of a basic parametric amplifier

Now we deduce the expression for the variable capacitance of the varactor diode of the parametric amplifier. We consider the equivalent circuit of parametric amplifier shown in figure 2.5-

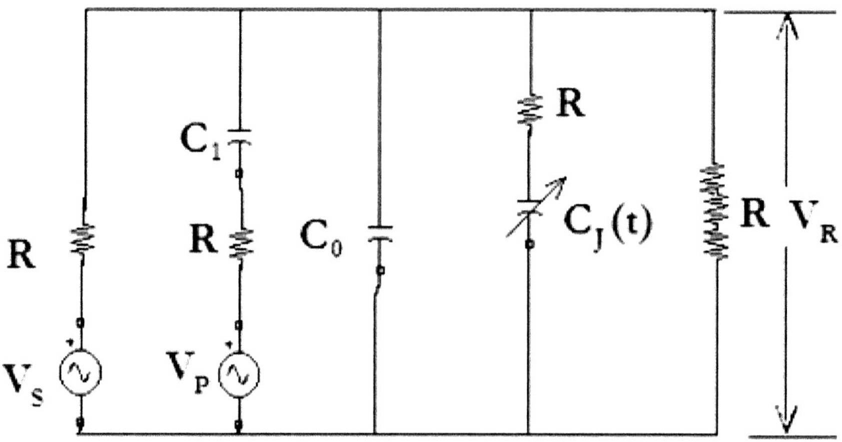

Fig 2.5: Equivalent circuit of a parametric amplifier

When a pump voltage $V_P = V_p \sin\omega_p t$ and a small signal voltage $V_S = V_S \sin\omega_S t$, where $V_S \ll V_P$ and $|V_S| \ll$ dc reverse bias voltage magnitude $|V_R|$, are applied simultaneously to time varying non-linear capacitance $C_j(t)$ of a varactor diode, the current through the diode is

$$i = \frac{dQ(v)}{dt} = \frac{dQ(v_p + v_s)}{dt}$$

(2.1)

Expanding $Q(V_P + V_S)$ in Taylor series about the small signal voltage $V_S = 0$ for $V_S \ll V_P$

$$Q(v_P + v_s) \approx Q(v_P) + \left.\frac{\partial Q}{\partial v}\right|_{v_s \to 0}$$

Therefore

$$i = \frac{dQ(v_P)}{dt} + \frac{d}{dt}\left(\left.\frac{\partial Q}{\partial V}\right|_{v_s \to 0} \cdot v_s\right)$$

(2.2)

This shows that the diode current is given by

$$i = \frac{dQ(v_P)}{dt} + \frac{d}{dt}\left(C_j(t) v_s\right)$$

(2.3)

And the junction capacitance is

$$C_j(t) = C_0\left[1 + \frac{V_R + V_p \sin \omega_p t + V_s \sin \omega_s t}{V_B}\right]^{-n}$$

(2.4)

For a linearly graded junction, $n=1/3$ and since $|V_s| << |V_p|$, $C_j(t)$ can be expanded in a harmonics series

$$C_j = C_0 - C_j \sin \omega_p t$$

$$(2.5)$$

This time varying capacitance is utilized for parametric amplifications.
The voltage variable junction capacitance given as when reverse biased as

$$C = C_0 (1 - V/V_0)^{-}$$

$$(2.6)$$

2.2 Parametric Up-Converter

Figure2.6 shows an equivalent circuit of a parametric up-converter in which a pump voltage at frequency f_p and asignal voltage at frequency at f_s are applied through respective tuned circuits to the varactor diode. The output power is taken from the idler circuit at either the lower sideband frequency $f_i = f_p - f_s$. or at the upper side frequency $f_i = f_p + f_s$. physically a power is transmitted from the pumping source to the idler circuit to achieve power gain with low noise. The series tuned circuit allow only currents with respective frequencies, f_s, f_p, and f_i in each loop. The circuit losses are small compared to the loss in the diode resistance R_s and external R_f and R_L. For maximum gain for a lossless $(R_s=0)$ diode is $G_m = w_i/w_s$.

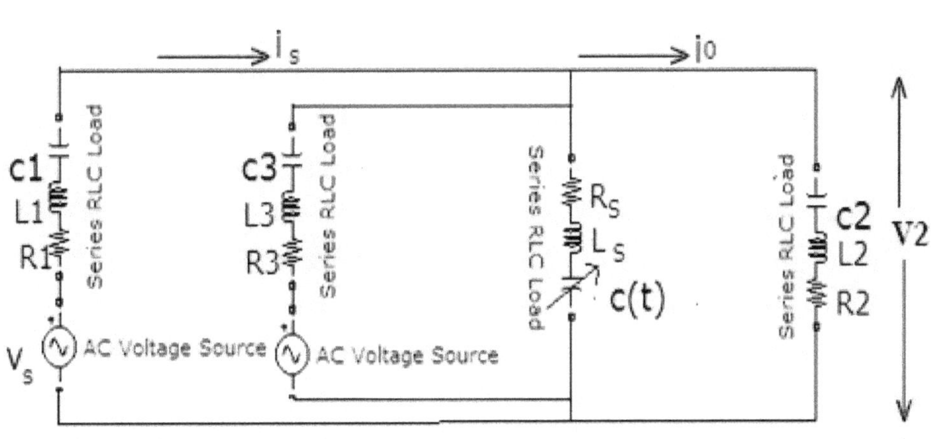

Fig 2.6: Parametric up-converter circuit

2.3 Advantages and limitation of Parametric Amplifier:

Parametric amplifiers have following advantages and limitations-

1. Noise figure: because of minimum resistive element thermal noise in parametric amplifier is very less compare to that of transistor amplifier. Typically, noise figure is in the range 1 to 2 dB.
2. Frequency: The upper frequency limit (40 to 200 GHz) is set by the difficulty of obtaining a source power at the pump frequency and by the frequency at which the varactor capacitance to be pumped the lower frequency limit is set by the cutoff frequency of the microwave components used in the circuit.
3. Bandwidth: Bandwidth of the parametric amplifier is small due to the presence of tuned circuits. Bandwidth can be increased by the stagger tuning.
4. Gain: The gain is limited (20 to 80 dB) by the stability of the pump source and the time varying capacitance.

Because of its low noise parametric amplifier are used in space communication system, radio telescopes and Tropo-receiver.

2.4 Fundamentals of Parametric Amplifiers:

To understand the operation of one of the forms of the parametric, amplifier, consider an LC circuit oscillating at its natural frequency, If the capacitor plates are physically pulled apart at the instant of time when the voltage between them is at its positive maximum, then work is done on the capacitor since a force must be applied to separate the plates. This work, or energy addition, appears as an increase in the voltage across the capacitor. Since V = q/C and the charge q remains constant, voltage is inversely proportional to capacitance. Since the capacitance has been reduced by the pulling apart of the plates, voltage across them has increased proportionately. The plates are now returned to their initial separation just as the voltage between them passes through zero, which involves no work. As the voltage passes through the negative maximum, the plates are pushed apart, and voltage increases once again. The process is repeated regularly, so that energy is taken from the "pump" source and added to the signal, at the signal frequency; amplification will take place if an input circuit and a load are connected. In practice, the capacitance is varied electronically (as could be the inductance). Thus the reactance variation can be made at a much faster rate than by mechanical means, and it is also sinusoidal rather than a square wave.

Comparing the principles of the parametric amplifier With those of more conventional amplifiers we see that the basic difference lies in use of a variable reactance (and an ac power-supply), by the former, and a variable resistance (and a dc power supply) by the latter. As an example, in an ordinary transistor amplifier, changes in base current cause changes in collector current when the collector supply voltage is constant; it may be said that the collector resistance is being changed.

The basic parametric amplifier just described requires the capacitance variation to occur at a pump frequency that is exactly twice the resonant frequency of the tuned circuit, and hence twice the signal frequency. It is thus phase-sensitive; this is a property that sometimes limits its usefulness. This mode of operation is called the Degenerate Mode, and it may also be shown that the amplifier is a negative-resistance one.

2.5 Basics of Parametric Amplifier:

If the pump frequency is other than twice the signal frequency, beating between the two will occur, and a difference signal, called the idler frequency, will appear. The amplitude of this idler signal is equal to the amplitude of the output signal, and its presence is an automatic consequence of using a pump frequency such that $f_p \neq 2f_s$. This means that if the idler signal is suppressed, the amplifier will have no gain.

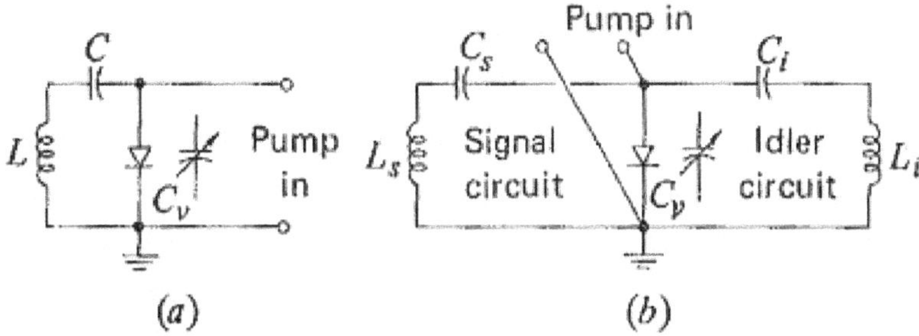

Fig 2.7 a) Degenerate Parametric Amplifier, b) Nondegenerate Parametric Amplifier

Figure 2.7 shows two simple parametric amplifier circuits. In the basic diagram Figure 2.7 (a) degenerate operation takes place, whereas for Figure 2.7 (b) fp ≠ 2fs, and the pumping is called non degenerate. An idler circuit is necessary for amplification to take place, and one is provided. The pump frequency tuned circuit has been left out in each case for the sake of simplicity. Note that nothing prevents us from taking the output at the idler frequency, and in fact there are a number of advantages in doing this.

The non degenerate parametric amplifier, like the degenerate one, produces gain, with the pump source being a net supplier of energy to the tank circuit. This can only be proved mathematically, with the aid of the Manley-Rowe relations. These show that substantial gain is available from this parametric amplifier, in which the pump frequency has no special relationship to the signal frequency (except to be higher, as a general rule). This still holds if sine-wave pumping is used, and it also applies if the output is at the idler frequency.

In the non degenerate parametric amplifier, the energy taken from the pumping source is transformed into added signal-frequency and idler-frequency energy and divides equally 'between the two tuned circuits. An amplified output may thus be obtained at either frequency, raising the possibility of frequency conversion with gain. In fact, two different types of converters are possible. If the pump frequency is much higher than the signal frequency, then the idler frequency fi, which is given by fi = fp – fs, will be much higher than fs, and the circuit is called an upconversion. If the pump frequency is only slightly higher, fi will be legs than fs, and a down converter, which is rather similar to the mixer in an ordinary radio receiver, will result.

2.6 Advantages and Disadvantages of Parametric Amplifier

Following are advantages of Parametric amplifier:
· Noise Figure: Because of minimum resistive elements, thermal noise in parametric amplifier is very less in comparison to transistor amplifier. Hence noise figure is less and will be in the range 1-2 dB.

· Frequency Range: The upper freqency limit (about 40 to 200GHz) is set by the difficulty of obtaining a source power at pump frequency and also by the frequency at which the varactor capacitance can be pumped. The lower frequency limit is set by the cut-off frequency of the microwave components used in circuit

· Bacause of its low noise, parametric smplifiers are used in space communications systems, tropo-receivers and radio telescopes.

Following are disadvantages of Parametric amplifier:

· Bandwidth: Parametric amplyfier bandwidth is small due to the presence of tuned circuits. Bandwidth can be increased by stagger tuning.

· Gain: It is limited by the stabilities of pump source and the time varying capacitance. It is usually in the rane of 20 to 80 dB.

III
CHAPTER 3: TYPES OF PARAMETRIC AMPLIFIER:

CHAPTER 3: PARAMETRIC AMPLIFIER TYPES:

3.1 Introduction:

The basic Parametric Amplifier Types have already been discussed in detail, but several others also exist. They differ from one another in the variable reactance used, the bandwidth required and the output frequency (signal or idler). Various other characteristics of Parametric Amplifier Types must also now be discussed, such as practical circuits, their performance and advantages, and lastly the important noise performance.

3.2 Amplifier Types:

When classifying parametric amplifiers, the first thing to decide is the device whose parameter will be varied. This is now always a varactor, whose capacitance is varied, but u variable inductance can also be used. Indeed, the first Parametric Amplifier Types, using an RF magnetic field to pump a small ferrite disk. Such amplifiers are no longer used, mainly because their noise figures do not compare with those available from varactor amplifiers.

Parametric Amplifier Types (or paramps) may be divided into two main groups; negative-resistance and positive-resistance. The upper-side band up-converter is the only useful member of the second group. Its output is taken at the idler frequency fi = fp + fs, and the pump frequency is less than signal frequency. The resulting amplifier has low gain, but a high pumping frequency is not required. This amplifier is most useful at the highest frequencies, for which it was developed.

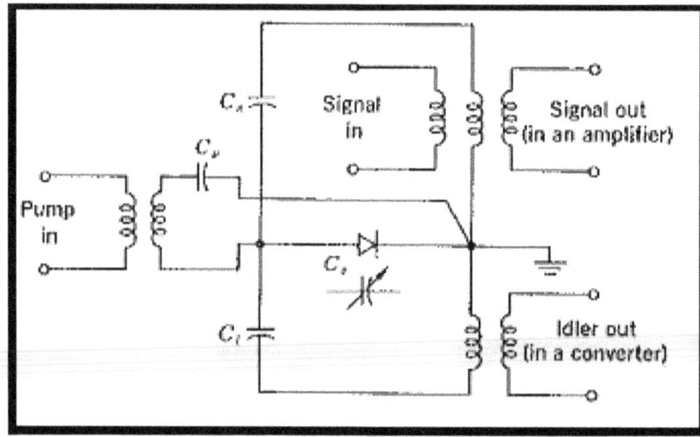

Fig 3.1 Parametric Amplifier

Negative-resistance paramps are either straight-out amplifiers (fo = fi) or lower-sideband converters. If the output is taken at the idler frequency, we have the two-port lower-sideband up-converter. Such a circuit is shown in Figure 3.1. The lower-sideband down-converter is in the same category. The output is still taken at the idler frequency, but this is now lower than the signal frequency. Both these amplifiers are nondegenerate.

The (straight-out) amplifier may be degenerate or not, depending on whether pump frequency is twice signal frequency. The two types share the disadvantage of being one-port (two-terminal) amplifiers. The nondegenerate amplifier is the one in which the pump frequency is (much) higher than the signal frequency but is quite unrelated to it. The circuit of Figure 3.1 also applies here.

Any paramp can belong to one of two broad classes. First there are narrowband amplifiers using a varactor diode that is part of a tuned circuit. Paramps can be wideband, in which case a number of diodes are used as part of a traveling-wave structure.

3.3 Narrowband Amplifiers:

The negative-resistance Parametric Amplifier Types almost always used in practice. The most commonly used types are the nondegenerate one-port amplifier and the two-port lower-sideband up-converter, in that order. The circuit of Figure 3.1 could be either type, depending on where the output is taken. The one-port amplifier may suffer from a lack of stability and low gain due mainly to the fact that the output is taken at the input frequency. On the other hand, the pump power is low and so is noise, and the amplifier can be made small, rugged and inexpensive.

Undoubtedly the fundamental drawback of this amplifier, as it stands, is that the input and output terminals are in parallel, as shown in Figure 3.1. This applies to all two-terminal amplifiers. If such an amplifier is followed by a relatively noisy stage such as a mixer, then the noise from the mixer, present at the output of the parametric amplifier, will find its way to the amplifier's input. therefore be re-amplified, and the noise performance will suffer.

In order to overcome this difficulty, a circulator is used. The four-terminal version of the Y stripline circulator is particularly suitable. The arrangement is then identical with the paramp replacing the tunnel diode amplifier shown there. The output of the antenna feeds the parametric amplifier, whose output can go only to the mixer. Any noise present at the input of the mixer can be coupled neither to the paramp nor to the antenna; it goes only to the matched termination. The circulator itself can generate some noise, but this may be reduced with proper techniques (such as cooling).

If the output is taken at the idler frequency (in Figure 3.1), a two-port lowersideband up-converter results, for which a circulator is not required. It has been shown that this type of amplifier is capable of a very low noise figure if fi/ fs is in excess of about 10. In fact, as this ratio increases, noise figure is lowered, but there are two limitations. The first is the complexity and/or lack of suitably powerful pump sources at millimeter wavelengths, which means that this amplifier is unlikely to be used above X band. The second limitation is the very narrow bandwidth available for minimum noise conditions. The result of all these considerations is that the nondegenerate one-port amplifier (with circulator) is most likely to be used for low-noise narrowband applications.

3.4 *Traveling-wave Diode Amplifiers:*

All the Parametric Amplifier Types so far described use cavity or coaxial resonators as tuned circuits. Since such resonators have high Q's and therefore narrow bandwidths; parametric amplifiers using them are anything but broadband; the available literature does not describe any such amplifier exceeding a bandwidth of 10 percent. However, it is possible to use traveling-wave structures for parametric amplifiers to provide bandwidths as large as 50 percent of the center frequency, with other properties comparable to those of narrowband amplifiers.

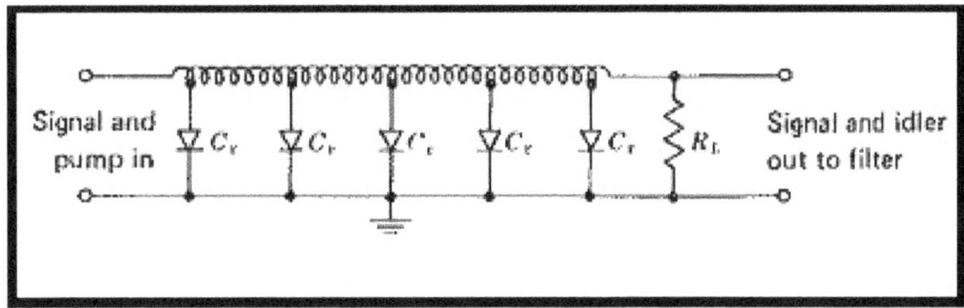

Fig 3.2 Travelling wave parametric amplifier

As shown in Figure 3.2, a typical traveling-wave amplifier employs a multistage low-pass filter, consisting of either a transmission line or lumped inductances, with suitably pumped shunt varactor diodes providing the shunt capacitances. The signal and pump frequencies are applied at the input end of the circuit, and the required output is taken from the other end. If the filter is correctly terminated at the desired output frequency, this will not be reflected back to the input, and thus unilateral operation is obtained, even for a negative-resistance amplifier without a circulator. The only real disadvantage is a lower gain than with narrowband amplifiers.

In order to obtain useful amplification, the pump, signal and idler frequencies must all fall within the bandpass of the filter, whereas the sum of the signal and the pump frequencies must fall outside the bandpass. This suggests that the pump frequency must not be very much higher than the signal frequency, or filtering will be difficult. As the wave progresses along the filter (lumped or transmission-line), the signal and idler voltages grow at the expense of the pumping signal. Although this power conversion becomes more complete as the length of the line is increased, the growth rate reduces. Maximum gain is achieved for a certain optimum length of line (or number of lumped sections), particularly as ohmic losses increase with the length.

3.5 Noise Cooling:

The noise figures of practical parametric amplifiers are extremely low, a very close second only to those of cooled multilevel masers, The reason for such low noise is that the variable transconductance used in the amplifying process is reactive, rather than resistive as in the more orthodox amplifiers. Once noise contributions due to associated circuitry (such as the circulator) have been minimized, the only noise source in the parametric amplifier is the base resistance, sometimes called the spreading resistance. This being the case, it seems that cooling the paramp and associated circuitry should have the effect of lowering its noise considerably.

Those paramps that are not operated at room temperature (290 K, or 17°C, is considered standard) may be cooled to about 230 K by using Peltier thermoelectric cooling. The next step is to use cryogenic cooling with liquid nitrogen (to 77 K) or with liquid helium (4.2 K). Cryogenic apparatus is outside the scope of this book, although one system.

It must be emphasized that cooling is used with some Parametric Amplifier Types in an attempt to improve their performance; it is neither compulsory nor always employed. As a matter of fact, although the noise temperature improvement which results from cooling is significant, it is not as great as might be expected. It would appear that the spreading resistance is increased as temperature is lowered, perhaps because of a decrease in the mobility of the varactor's charge carriers. The point is uncertain, however, because measurements at extremely low temperatures are rather difficult to make.

3.6 Degenerate Parametric Aamplifier:

Principle of Operation When the signal and idler waves have identical frequencies, such a parametric amplifier is called a degenerate parametric amplifier and has a unique characteristic. Consider a swing driven by a person. During one-half cycle (left to right) of the swing, the person makes a full one cycle (up-down-up). The frequency of the driving person (pump) and that of the driven swing (signal) satisfy *wp=2ws*. Figure 3.4 is an equivalent LCR circuit of the swing, in which the driving action of the person is represented by the nonlinear capacitor.

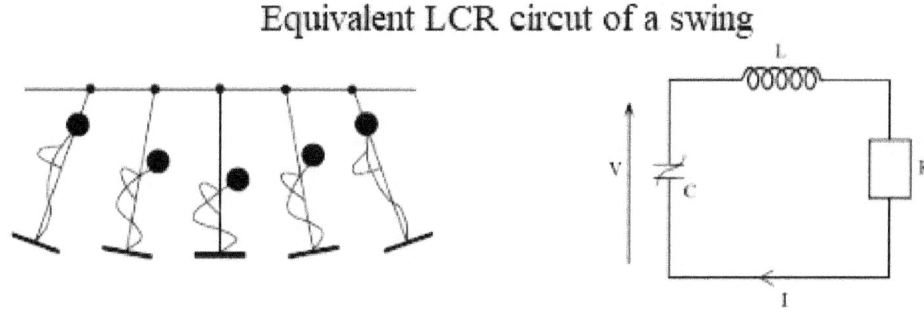

Fig 3.4 A swing driven by a person and an equivalent circuit

In the rarely used degenerate case, signal and idler waves are identical not only in frequency but also in polarization, i.e., they are indistinguishable. There is therefore only a signal amplitude ?1 and a pump amplitude ?2, and no idler. The signal wavelength is then exactly twice the pump wavelength. The interaction is described with the equations

?/??(?1)=??1∗?2exp (−?Δ??)
?/??(?2)=−?|?1|2exp (+?Δ??)
with Δ?=?2−2?1

Here, the amplification is phase sensitive. For example, signal amplification occurs (for zero phase mismatch) if the signal and pump amplitudes are real and positive, or there is signal deamplification when the sign of the pump amplitude is changed. The direction of energy transfer is governed by the complex phase of the term ?12?2∗.

Phase-sensitive amplification provides a mechanism for producing so-called squeezed states of light (e.g. a squeezed vacuum), and also in principle it allows one to avoid excess amplifier noise, i.e., to keep the noise figure near 1. However, the need to maintain a fixed phase relationship between pump and signal makes this kind of optical amplification too inconvenient e.g. for use in optical fiber communications.

3.7 Nondegenerate Parametric Amplifier:

Here, we consider parametric amplification based on a ?(2) nonlinearity in a nonlinear crystal material such as LiNbO3 or lithium triborate (LBO).

In the nondegenerate case, there is an interaction between three distinct light waves, the angular frequencies of which are ?1, ?2, and ?3 (with the indices in the order of the frequency values):

- The pump wave has the frequency ?3.
- The signal wave has the frequency ?2.
- A so-called idler wave with the frequency ?1 is generated in the interaction.

For reasons of energy conservation, the relation ?3=?1+?2 must hold. The idler frequency ?1 is often below the signal frequency ?2, but it can also be higher than that; in any case, both signal and idler frequency are below the pump frequency.

Signal and idler generally have different optical frequencies, but even the case of equal frequencies may be considered as degenerate if the two waves can still be distinguished through different polarization directions.

Essentially, the amplification process implies that some of the pump photons are converted to signal and idler photons. More precisely, for each disappearing pump photon, one signal photon and one idler photon is generated. Although the idler photons leaving the nonlinear crystal are often not used, there are essential in the amplification process: for a material with strong absorption of the idler wave, the amplifier performance can be strongly degraded.

3.8 Phase Sensitive Amplifier:

Changing the pump phase from $\varphi = 0$ to $\varphi = \pi$ corresponds to shifting the capacitance modulation by half a pump period, which is equivalent to one-quarter signal period. That is, one quadrature amplitude of the signal wave corresponding to the $\varphi = 0$ solution is amplified by a gain coefficient $2\alpha = \omega_0 \Delta C / 2C_0 - R/L$ but the other quadrature amplitude corresponding to the $\varphi = \pi$ solution is deamplified by an attenuation coefficient $2\alpha' = \omega_0 \Delta C / 2C_0 - R/L$. This type of operation is called a phase sensitive amplifier.

3.9 Parametric Amplification in Fibers:

Due to the centrosymmetric nature of the material, glass fibers do not exhibit a ?(2) nonlinearity (unless under certain circumstances, for example when fibers are "poled" with a strong electric field). However, parametric amplification can also occur as a result of the ?(3) nonlinearity. In that case, four different frequencies can be involved: two pump frequencies, a signal frequency, and an idler frequency. A frequent case is that of partial degeneracy, where one has only a single pump wave.

The interaction is somewhat complicated because the optical phases of signal and idler are influenced both via cross-phase modulation (XPM) and the chromatic dispersion of the fiber. (For strong signals, self-phase modulation occurs in addition.) Parametric amplification is obtained only within some wavelength range around the pump wavelength. That range can be fairly wide when the chromatic dispersion is weak, and its width depends on the pump power.

3.10 Saturation gain of parametric amplifier:

When power is transferred from the pump to the signal, the optical-pump power cannot sustain the exponential growth of the gain, saturation occurs. The relative magnitudes of the pump and signal/idler powers will affect the flow of power between them due to the nonlinear phase-matching condition.

This saturation power can be interpreted as the input signal power required for the gain G0 to convert the whole pump to the signal and idler waves. These equations are only valid for the single wavelength when the pump is totally converted and under the assumption of three waves only.

The signal input powers are normalized to the saturated gain at the gain-peak wavelength according to Ps0/Psat,max. As the input power increases, the peak gain shifts toward the pump wavelength, because the nonlinear phase matching is altered as the signal/idler powers increase. The pump is completely converted at $\lambda n = 0.5$. The peak gain is shifted to that wavelength of higher input power and at other wavelengths, the power is periodically exchanged between the signal/idler and optical pump with length. This also explains the dramatic change in gain which is reduced at higher normalized input powers.

3.11 Noise in Amplifiers:

This section will discuss the noise properties of parametric amplifiers and in particular PSAs. We will consider both the semi-classical approach and the quantum mechanical.

Semi-classical model

The semi-classical model of light-matter interaction means that one has a classical field formulation, but a quantum mechanical model of matter. When modeling noise in optical amplification, the amplifier has spontaneously emitted photons that can be treated as additive noise and that have (at the amplifier input) a power spectral density of half a photon per mode.

From this assumption, a lot of well-known results follow; for example, the shot noise power spectral density and the familiar result for amplifier noise figures. The NF is defined as the ratio of input to output SNR (in the electrical domain, after ideal photodetection) of an optical amplifier. It is also a measure of the amount of spontaneous emission noise an amplifier adds to a signal.

Phase-insensitive amplifiers (PIA) have a noise figure of NFPIA = 2–1/G, approaching 3 dB for high gain. Parametric amplifiers have, in phase-sensitive operation, a noise figure of NFPSA = 1 (gain is 0 dB) instead, because the quantum noise is unevenly between the adjoining quadratures (which is known as squeezing). The PSA, however, have a NF of 1/2 (–3 dB) if only the signal wave is considered and the idler contains a conjugate signal copy. This comes from the 6 dB difference in gain between PIA and PSA as we saw above and ultimately from the coherent superposition. This means that a PSA and a PIA giving the same gain will have ASE noise floors that differ by 6 dB.

Quantum theory

A full noise theory for the PSA must be based on quantum mechanics, and we sketch a derivation here. In quantum field theory, the two quadratures of a mode are described by operators a1,2 that must obey the commutator relation [a1, a2] = i/2. The commutation between two operators implies a Heisenberg uncertainty relation between the two modes. A linear amplifier with gain G1,2 for the respective quadratures is described by

b1=G1a1+F1E19

b2=G2a2+F2E20

where the added noise field operators F1,2 are necessary if the commutation relation should hold also for the output modes b1,2. It is easy to see that the absence of these noise fields would lead to contradictions, e.g., arbitrarily small uncertainties violating the Heisenberg uncertainty relation. Thus, every amplifier must have these additive fields. Applying the commutation relation to the output fields gives a relation on the noise field operators as

F1F2=i21–G1G2E21

The Robertson uncertainty relation states that if two operators commute with a commutator x, their uncertainty product is |x|2. The uncertainty for F1,2 is then

ΔF12ΔF22=141–G1G22E22

The noise figure is then

NFPSA=a12a22Δa12Δa22Δb12Δb22b12b12=1+ΔF12ΔF22Δb22G1G2Δa12Δa22=1+1–1G1G22E23

For a PSA, the two quadratures' gain obey G1G2 = 1, and this then reduces to NFPSA = 1. For the PIA, G1 = G2 = G, and the derivation can be simplified by noting that the gain is the same for both quadratures, so that

NFPIA=1+ΔF2GΔa2=1+1–1G=2–1GE24

This summarizes the well-known properties of the noise figures for amplifiers. More detailed discussions on the quantum mechanical properties of parametric processes (including, for example, the noise for the phase conjugation and Bragg scattering processes) can be found in the works of McKinstrie [10, 11].

It should also be mentioned that other noise sources than the fundamental quantum noise discussed above contribute to parametric amplifiers, e.g., noise from the Raman effect, pump-induced noise, and excess ASE noise from the pump boosters which can make it difficult to get closer than 1 dB within the quantum noise figure limit in experiments.

IV
CHAPTER 4: NETWORK FUNCTION & S-PARAMETERS

CHAPTER 4: NETWORK FUNCTION & S-PARAMETERS

4.1 Introduction:

The transfer function is used to describe network which have at least two ports. Using transfer function a system can be characterized by the roots of its characteristic equation and the stability of the system can be described in terms of these roots of the transfer equation. In this chapter we first solve the general second order differential equation of an electronic circuit with internal excitation, then after describing the network function, zero and poles, we explain the stability in terms of zero and poles and give a brief idea of s-parameters.

Linear networks, or nonlinear networks operating with signals sufficiently small to cause the networks to respond in a linear manner, can be completely characterized by parameters measured at the network terminals (ports) without regard to the contents of the networks. Once the parameters of a network have been determined, its behavior in any external environment can be predicted, again without regard to the contents of the network. S-parameters are important in microwave design because they are easier to measure and work with at high frequencies than other kinds of parameters. They are conceptually simple, analytically convenient, and capable of providing a great insight into a measurement or design problem. To show how s-parameters ease microwave design, and how you can best take advantage of their abilities, this application note describes s-parameters and flow graphs, and relates them to more familiar concepts such as transducer power gain and voltage gain. Data obtained with a network analyzer is used to illustrate amplifier design.

Although a network may have any number of ports, network parameters can be explained most easily by considering a network with only two ports, an input port and an output port, like the network shown in Figure 1. To characterize the performance of such a network, any of several parameter sets can be used, each of which has certain advantages. Each parameter set is related to a set of four variables associated with the two-port model. Two of these variables represent the excitation of the network (independent variables), and the remaining two represent the response of the network to the excitation (dependent variables). If the network of Fig. 1 is excited by voltage sources V1 and V2, the network currents I1 and I 2 will be related by the following equations (assuming the network behaves linearly):

I1=y1V11+y12V2

and I2=y21V1+y22V2

In this case, with port voltages selected as independent variables and port currents taken as dependent variables, the relating parameters are called short-circuit admittance parameters, or y-parameters. In the absence of additional information, four measurements are required to determine the four parameters y11, y12, y21, y22. Each measurement is made with one port of the network excited by a voltage source while the other port is short circuited. For example, y21, the forward transadmittance, is the ratio of the current at port 2 to the voltage at port 1 with port 2 short circuited, i.e y21=I2/V1.

If other independent and dependent variables had been chosen, the network would have been described, as before, by two linear equations similar to equations 1 and 2, except that the variables and the parameters describing their relationships would be different. However, all parameter sets contain the same information about a network, and it is always possible to calculate any set in terms of any other set. "Scattering parameters," which are commonly referred to as s-parameters, are a parameter set that relates to the traveling waves that are scattered or reflected when an n-port network is inserted into a transmission line.

The ease with which scattering parameters can be measured makes them especially well suited for describing transistors and other active devices. Measuring most other parameters calls for the input and output of the device to be successively opened and short circuited. This can be hard to do, especially at RF frequencies where lead inductance and capacitance make short and open circuits difficult to obtain. At higher frequencies these measurements typically require tuning stubs, separately adjusted at each measurement frequency, to reflect short or open circuit conditions to the device terminals. Not only is this inconvenient and tedious, but a tuning stub shunting the input or output may cause a transistor to oscillate, making the measurement invalid. S-parameters, on the other hand, are usually measured with the device imbedded between a 50 Ω load and source, and there is very little chance for oscillations to occur.

Another important advantage of s-parameters stems from the fact that traveling waves, unlike terminal voltages and currents, do not vary in magnitude at points along a lossless transmission line. This means that scattering parameters can be measured on a device located at some distance from the measurement transducers, provided that the measuring device and the transducers are connected by low-loss transmission lines.

4.2 Second Order Differential Equation; Internal Excitation

A second order differential equation with constant coefficient may be written in general form

$$a_0 \frac{d^2 i}{d t^2} + a_1 \frac{d i}{d t} + a_2 i = 0$$

4.1

The solution of this equation must be of such form that the solution, its first derivative and its second derivative – each multiplied by a constant coefficient – add to zero. To satisfying this requirement the three terms must be of the same form, differing only in their coefficients. Let us assume the solution is

$$i(t) = k e^{S_n t} = k e^{\sigma_n t + j \omega_n t}$$

4.2

Where k and s are constants which may be real, imaginary, or complex. Substituting the exponential solution in equation 4.1 gives

$$a_0 k e^{S t} + a_1 S k e^{S t} + a_2 k e^{S t} = 0$$

4.3

As $ke^{st} \neq 0$ for finite t,

$$a\,S^{2} - a\,S - a = 0$$

$$4.4$$

This equation is the characteristic equation. It is satisfied by the two roots given by the quadratic formula

$$S_{1}\,S_{2} = -\frac{a}{2a} = 1/2a\,\sqrt{a^{2} - 4a\,a}$$

$$4.5$$

Hence the two solutions are

$$i_{1} = k_{1}\,e^{S_{1}} \qquad \text{and} \qquad i_{2} = k_{2}\,e^{S_{2}}$$

$$4.6$$

Now, if i_1 and i_2 are each solutions of the differential equation of Eq. 4.1, the sum of these solutions, Is also a solution

Hence

$i_3 = i_1 + i_2 \quad (4.7)$

Substituting Eq. 4.6 in Eq. 4.1 and rearranging we get

$$\left(a\frac{d^{2}i}{dt^{2}} - a\frac{di}{dt} - a\,i\right) - \left(a\frac{d^{2}i}{dt^{2}} - a\frac{di}{dt} - a\,i\right) = 0$$

$$4.8$$

The general solution of the differential equation is thus

$$i(t) = k_1 e^{S_1 t} + k_2 e^{S_2 t} = k_n e^{S_n t}$$

$$4.9$$

4.3 Network Function for Two-port Network

A function relating current or voltage at different part of the network called transfer function. It is found to be mathematically similar to the transform impedance function. These functions are called Network functions.

The transform impedance at a port has been defined as the ratio of the voltage transform to current transform for a network in the zero state (no initial condition) with no internal voltage or current sources except controlled sources. Thus we write

$$Z(s) = V(s)/I(s)$$

$$4.10$$

Similarly the transfer admittance is defined as the ratio

$$Y(s) = I(s)/V(s) = 1/Z(s)$$

$$4.11$$

The transfer function is used to describe network which have at least two ports, and these functions are computed under the same assumptions that are listed for driving-point function. In general the transfer function relates the transform of a quantity at one port to the transform of another quantity at another port. Thus transfer functions which have the following possible forms:

1. The ratio of one voltage to another voltage, or the voltage transfer ratio.
2. The ratio of one current to another current, or the current transfer ratio.
3. The ratio of one current to another voltage or one voltage to another current.

It is conventional, although not universal, to define transfer function or the network function as the ratio of an output quantity to an input quantity.

We observed that all the network functions have been quotients of polynomials in s having the general form-

$$N(S) = \frac{a_0 s^n + a_1 s^{n-1} + \cdots\cdots\cdots\cdots + a_{n-1} s^1 + a_n}{b_0 s^m + b_1 s^{m-1} + \cdots\cdots\cdots\cdots + b_{n-1} s^1 + b_m}$$

$$4.12$$

Which is a rational function of s (n and m are integers). In the equation n is the degree of the numerator polynomial, and m is the degree of the denominator polynomial.

4.4 Poles and Zeros of Network Function

From equation 4.12 we have shown that all the network functions have been quotients of polynomials in s,

$$N(S) = \frac{p(s)}{q(s)} = \frac{a_0 s^n + a_1 s^{n-1} + \cdots\cdots\cdots + a_{n-1} s^1 + a_n}{b_0 s^m + b_1 s^{m-1} + \cdots\cdots\cdots + b_{m-1} s^1 + b_m}$$

$$4.13$$

Where-

$$p(s) = a_0 s^n + a_1 s^{n-1} + \cdots\cdots\cdots + a_{n-1} s^1 + a_n$$

$$4.14$$

And

$$q(s) = b_0 s^m + b_1 s^{m-1} + \text{-----------} + b_{n-1} s^1 + b_n$$

4.15

Where the a and b coefficients are real and positive for network of passive element and no controlled sources.

Now the equation $P(s) = 0$ has n roots and $q(s)=0$ has m roots. Both $p(s)$ and $q(s)$ may be written as a product of linear factors involving these roots as

$$N(s) = \frac{(S - Z_1)(S - Z_2)\text{-----------}(S - Z_n)}{(S - P_1)(S - P_2)\text{-----------}(S - P_m)}$$

4.16

Where $N(s) = a_0/b_0$ is a constant known as the scalar factor, and $z_1, z_2 \text{........} z_n, p_1, p_2 \text{......} p_m$ are complex frequencies.

When the variable s has the values $z_1, z_2 \text{........} z_n$ *the* network function vanishes; such complex frequencies are known as the Zeros of the network function.

When s has values $p_1, p_2 \text{......} p_m$ the network function becomes infinite; such complex frequencies are the poles of the network function.

Factors (S-Zj) are known as zero factors; factor (S-Pj) is called pole factors.

Poles and zeros are very useful in describing network functions.

When *r* poles or zeros in equation 4.16 have the same value, the pole or zero is said to be of multiplicity *r*. If for any rational network function, poles and zeros at zero and infinity are taken into account in addition to finite poles and zeros, the total numbers of zeros are equal to the total numbers of poles.

4.5 *Restriction of location of Poles and Zeros in driving point function*

The following list provides the listing of restrictions of location of poles and zeros in driving point function-

1. The coefficient of polynomials $p(s)$ and $q(s)$ of the network function $N(s)$ must be real and positive.
2. Poles and zeros, if complex or imaginary, must occur in conjugate pairs.

3. The real part of all poles and zeros must be zero or negative.
4. The polynomial $p(s)$ and $q(s)$ cannot have any missing term between those of highest and lowest order values unless all even order or all order terms are missing.
5. The degree of $p(s)$ and $q(s)$ may differ by zero or one only.
6. The lowest degree in $p(s)$ and $q(s)$ may differ in degree by at the most one.

4.6 Stability in terms of Zero and Poles

Poles and zeros are the lifeblood of a function. Without zeros and poles the function becomes dull, drab, grubby constant-a function which does not change under any conditions. Poles and zeros are the critical frequencies, at poles network function becomes infinite and at zeros network function becomes zero. At other complex frequencies, the network function has a finite, nonzero value.

We know that the solution of a differential equation (4.1) for a network can be written as,

$$i(t) = k e^{St} = k e^{\sigma t - j\omega t}$$

4.17

Where

$$S = \sigma - j\omega$$

4.18

In terms of damping ratio ξ and the undamped natural frequency w_n, the poles and zeros of the last equation of transfer function will have the following forms,

$$S_n = -\zeta\omega_n \pm j\omega_n\sqrt{1-\zeta^2} \qquad ; \ \zeta < 1 \qquad\qquad (4.19)$$

$$S_n = -\zeta\omega_n \pm j\omega_n\sqrt{\zeta^2-1} \qquad ; \ \zeta > 1 \qquad\qquad (4.20)$$

$$S_n = -\omega_n \qquad\qquad\qquad\qquad ; \ \zeta > 1 \qquad\qquad (4.21)$$

$$S_n = \pm j\omega_n \qquad\qquad\qquad\qquad ; \ \zeta = 0 \qquad\qquad (4.22)$$

The system is unstable if any of the root of its characteristic equation has real part greater then zero. This is equivalent to any of the eigen value of state matrix having real part greater than zero.

That means if σ greater than zero then the system is is said to be unstable, where $\sigma = -\xi w_n$. Thus if there is no damping on the system, that means $\xi = 0$, the roots of the equation are imaginary only. The system which roots are only imaginary can be described as an unstable system.

The system composed of passive networks is stable in the sense that the poles of the network functions describing them are excluded from the right half of the s plane. That active network which containing controlled sources is not necessarily stable.

For an example if we consider a network with a controlled source which voltage is related to V_2 by a positive constant A. The corresponding figure is given below,

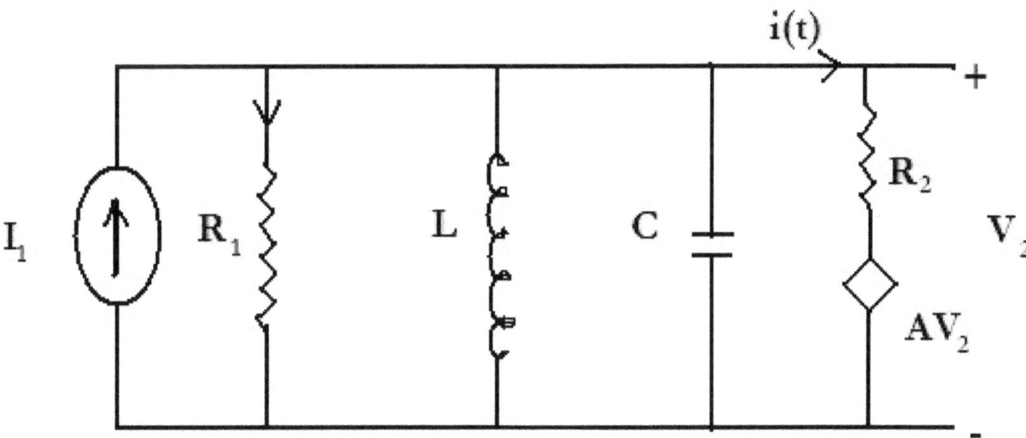

Fig 4.1 Network with a controlled source

Routine analysis of the network gives the transfer function

$$\frac{V_2}{I_1} = \frac{1}{C} \cdot \frac{s}{s^2 + [(1/R_1 C) + (1-A)/(R_2 C)]s + 1/LC}$$

4.23

If we specify the values for the elements by letting $R_1=1/2, R_2=1, L=1/2, and C=1$, then equation 4.23 becomes

$$\frac{V_2}{I_1} = \frac{s}{s^2 + (3-A)s + 2}$$

4.24

So the poles locations are determined by the constant A, and also that the poles will migrate in the s plane as A increase from 0 to vary large value. Now the root locus plots we see that the poles are located on the negative real axis for $A=0$. As A increases, the poles moves towards each other, meeting at $S=-\sqrt{2}$. Thereafter the locus is a circle for the range of values $3-22 \le A \le 3+2\sqrt{2}$. When A=3, the poles are located on the imaginary axis.

For A>3+2√2, 4.25

the poles are again on the real axis, but remain in the right half of the s plane-on moving towards zero and the other toward infinity. So clearly the poles pass the critical boundary which is the imaginary axis for a range of values of a, and the network output is thus capable of being stable, oscillatory, or unstable. Thus when $A>3$, the output oscillate with an amplitude which increases with time without limit.

Hence we state that an active network is stable if the transfer function relating Output to input has poles which are confined to the left half plane and imaginary axis, and strictly stable if the poles are in the left half plane only. The system is marginally stable if all the Poles are on the imaginary axis.

Since stability is determined by poles location, we may state the necessary condition for stability in terms of a requirement on the denominator polynomial of the transfer function relating output to input. Let the polynomial be

$$B(s) = b_n s^n - b s - b s \quad \text{------------} \quad b_1 s - b_0$$

$$4.26$$

According to Routh-Hurwith criterion of stability of network, the stability of network can be observed utilizing the following steps-

1. The array is to be constructed first.
2. Two rows of coefficient are formed; first row containing even numbered coefficients and the second row odd numbered coefficients.
3. The array is to be completed.

Now from the equation 4.26, if we consider m=5, the array will contain (m+1) i.e. 6 rows.

Array

$$
\begin{array}{llll}
S^5 & b_0 & b_2 & b_4 \\
S^4 & b_1 & b_3 & b_5 \\
S^3 & c_1 & c_2 & \\
S^2 & d_1 & d & \\
S^1 & e_1 & & \\
S^0 & f_1 & &
\end{array}
$$

$$4.27$$

Where

$$C_1 = \frac{\begin{vmatrix} b_2 & b_2 \\ b_1 & b_3 \end{vmatrix}}{b_1} = \frac{b_1 b_2 - b_2 b_3}{b_1} \qquad (4.28)$$

$$C_2 = \frac{\begin{vmatrix} b_2 & b_4 \\ b_1 & b_5 \end{vmatrix}}{b_1} = \frac{b_1 b_4 - b_2 b_5}{b_1} \qquad (4.29)$$

$$d_1 = \frac{\begin{vmatrix} b_1 & b_3 \\ c_1 & c_2 \end{vmatrix}}{c_1} = \frac{c_1 b_3 - b_1 c_2}{c_1} \qquad (4.30)$$

$$d_2 = \frac{\begin{vmatrix} b_1 & b_5 \\ c_1 & 0 \end{vmatrix}}{c_1} = \frac{b_5 c_1}{c_1} = b_5 \qquad (4.31)$$

$$e_1 = \frac{\begin{vmatrix} c_1 & c_2 \\ d_1 & d_2 \end{vmatrix}}{d_1} = \frac{c_2 d_1 - c_1 d_2}{d_1} \qquad (4.32)$$

$$f_1 = \frac{\begin{vmatrix} d_1 & d_2 \\ e_1 & 0 \end{vmatrix}}{e_1} = \frac{d_2 e_1}{e_1} = d_2 \qquad (4.33)$$

Now according to Routh-Hurwith criterion, the system is said to be stable, if and only if, there are no changes in signs of the first column of the array. This gives the roots with negative real parts and hence gives the condition of stability. So we can say that if there is a sign change in the first column of the array that means the roots with positive real parts, hence the system is totally unstable.

4.7 S-Parameters

S-parameters refer to the scattering matrix. The scattering matrix is a mathematical construct that quantifies how RF energy propagates through a multi-port network. The S-matrix is what allows us to accurately describe the properties of incredibly complicated networks as simple "black boxes". S-parameters are complex (magnitude and angle) because both the magnitude and phase of the input signal are changed by the network. S-parameters refer to RF "voltage out versus voltage in" in the most basic sense. S-parameters come in a matrix, with the number of rows and columns equal to the number of ports. S11 refers to the ratio of signal that reflects from port one for a signal incident on port one. Parameters along the diagonal of the S-matrix are referred to as reflection coefficients because they only refer to what happens at a single port, while off-diagonal S-parameters are referred to as transmission coefficients, because they refer to what happens from one port to another.

S-parameters describe the response of an N-port network to voltage signals at each port. The first number in the subscript refers to the responding port, while the second number refers to the incident port. Scattering parameters or S-parameters (the elements of a scattering matrix or S-matrix) describe the electrical behaviors of linear electrical networks when undergoing various steady state stimuli by electrical signals.

The scattering matrix is given as considering the two port black box circuit, we get

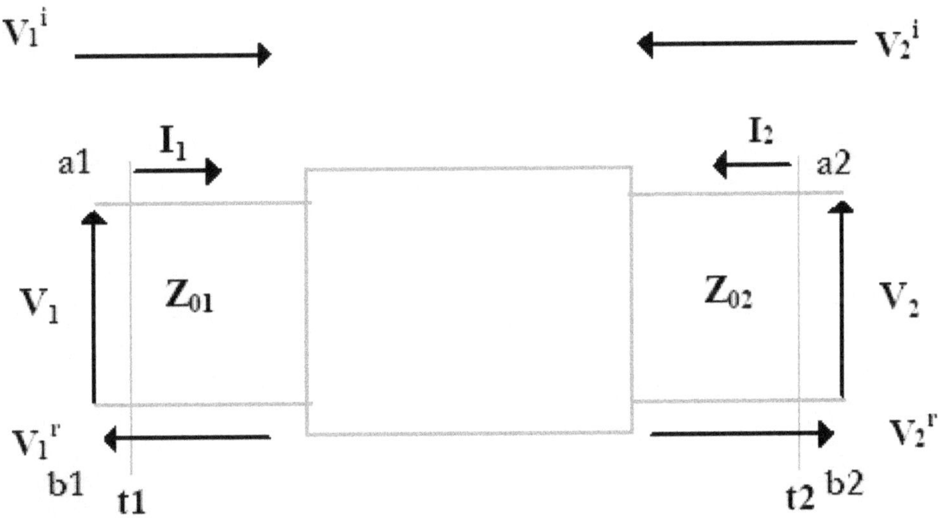

Fig 4.2: Two port network

Define normalized voltages as,

$$a_1 = \frac{V_1^i}{\sqrt{Z_{c1}}}$$

4.34

$$b_1 = \frac{V_1^i}{\sqrt{Z_{c1}}} \tag{4.35}$$

$$a_2 = \frac{V_2^i}{\sqrt{Z_{c1}}} \tag{4.36}$$

$$b_2 = \frac{V_2^i}{\sqrt{Z_{c1}}} \tag{4.37}$$

Outgoing voltage waves ∞ ingoing voltage waves. The scattering matrix is given as,

$$b_1 = S_{11}a_1 + S_{12}a_2$$
$$b_2 = S_{21}a_1 + S_{22}a_2$$

$$\begin{bmatrix} b_1 \\ b_2 \end{bmatrix} = \begin{bmatrix} S_{11} & S_{12} \\ S_{21} & S_{22} \end{bmatrix} \begin{bmatrix} a_1 \\ a_2 \end{bmatrix} \tag{4.38}$$

Measurement of $s11$ and $s22$:

(1) Apply input to Port 1, terminate at Port 2 with a Matched Load, i.e. $a2 = 0$.

$$S_{11} = \left.\frac{b_1}{a_1}\right)_{a_2=0}$$

Reflection coefficient at port 1 (match load at port 2).

$$S_{21} = \left.\frac{b_2}{a_1}\right)_{a_2=0}$$

Voltage transfer ratio at port 1 (match load at port 2).

Apply input to port 2, terminate at port 1 with matched load, $a1=0$.

$$S_{22} = \left.\frac{b_2}{a_2}\right)_{a_1=0}$$

Reflection coefficient at port 2 (match load at port 1).

$$S_{12} = \left.\frac{b_1}{a_2}\right)_{a_1=0}$$

Transfer ratio port 2 to port 1 (match load at port 1).

Hence we can state that-

1. S_{11} is the input port voltage reflection coefficient.
2. S_{12} is the reverse voltage gain.
3. S_{21} is the forward voltage gain.
4. S_{22} is the output port voltage reflection coefficient.

The reverse isolation parameter S_{12} determines the level of feedback from the output of an amplifier to the input and therefore influences its stability (its tendency to refrain from oscillation) together with the forward gain S_{21}.

S-parameters (or scattering parameters) are used to describe how energy can propagate through an electric network. S-Parameters are used to describe the relationship between different ports, when it becomes especially important to describe a network in terms of amplitude and phase versus frequencies, rather than voltages and currents. S-Parameters are used to show a complicated network as a simple black box, and to easily present what happens to the signal in that network.

The S-parameters can be saved e.g. as a S4P-file that contains all the combinations of the reflection and transmissions in a network, and this shows how the device under test behaves with a signal in both forward and reverse directions.

4.8 S-Parameters and Two-port Measurements

Network analyzers are the fundamental instrument for the characterization of the devices and components used in RF and microwave systems. Network analyzers were briefly introduced in the previous laboratory for their use in impedance matching; they now will be examined in more detail within the context of component measurement. Transfer functions are more naturally expressed in the Laplace or frequency domain, and swept frequency instruments, like network analyzers, can provide a direct measurement of these transfer functions by sweeping a signal source and a tuned receiver across a range of frequencies. Two-port measurements provide an explicit characterization of linear system blocks with a single input and a single output, by far the most common type of element. A two-port network could be as simple as a section of cable, or as complex as a complete transmitter-receiver link. In its simplest format, a reference excitation is applied to one port, and the response from the other port is recorded as a function of the sweep frequency. More complex elements with more than two ports can be characterized by extension, and the measurement techniques extend easily by simple multiplexing of the stimulus and response ports. Scattering parameters, or S-parameters for short, are the working language of network analyzers (NA). They provide a complete description of any linear, time-invariant element which then fully represents the behavior of that element within any system that it may be connected to. Scattering parameters involve phase information, and they are thus complex phasor quantities, and they are also frequency-dependent. Once known, they can be transformed into other network parameters for circuit design, optimization, or tuning.

An electrical port is a pair of terminals across which a unique voltage and current can be defined, and through which an electrical signal or power can flow. A two-terminal element such as a resistor, capacitor, or inductor is a one-port device. The characteristics of that element define a relationship between the port voltage and the port current, for example, $V = IR$, or $V = L \, dI/dt$. One of these variables say voltage, can be considered as a stimulus to the element, and the other variable, say current, can be considered as the response. The characteristics of the two-terminal element thus describe an electrical stimulus-response relationship.

A two-port device or network is the simplest electrical element with a unique input and output. A generic two-port network is illustrated in figure 1 below where the port variables of voltage and current are denoted in their more conventional circuit theory manner.

Because of the larger number of variables (now four), a two-port network requires a more elaborate method of characterization, and several matrix approaches exist for organizing this process. One such method is the impedance matrix, or Z-matrix. The Z-matrix representation of a two-port network can be thought of as having the two port currents, I1 and I 2 , be the independent stimuli, and the two port voltages, V1 and V2 , be the responses that arise from those stimuli.

Reversing the roles of the stimuli and responses gives an alternative representation, the admittance matrix, or Y-matrix.

Simple matrix algebra shows that the impedance and admittance matrices are inverses of each other, Y = Z–1. Numerous other representations are possible, each with different choices for the stimuli and responses. The more common ones are the G-, H-, and T- or ABCD-matrices, which are developed in other courses on linear network theory.

When dealing with high-frequency systems where the propagation of signals is better described by traveling waves, the choice of stimuli and responses needs to be modified. The stimuli are best described by waves that are incident upon the ports, and the responses are best described by waves that are reflected back from those same ports. Figure 2 illustrates the same two-port network as in figure 1, but with the port variables now labeled as an incident (in-going, +) and reflected (out-going, –) voltage waves.

4.9 Functions and principles of S-parameters:

As design frequencies now routinely go into the hundreds of MHz and tens of GHz range, conventional voltage and current measurements are not useful. However, scattering (s) parameters can fully characterize the RF component or path performance.

For engineers with experience focused from DC to several hundred megahertz, it is usually sufficient to characterize components by their voltage and current characteristics for much of the design effort. However, as designs now routinely go to much-higher frequencies, often into the tens of gigahertz, this characterization is impractical, inadequate, and even misleading.

Instead, a measurement and characterization metric called scattering parameters—often called S-parameters—is used. This FAQ will look at the basics and the need for S-parameters as well as their application and test. By their nature, S-parameters and what they represent is a complicated, math-intensive topic. We will only present the basics here.

Whether you call it RF or microwaves, measuring voltage or current at those higher frequencies is tough. Even if you do, the measured values have little immediate meaning since the RF world is one of "power" and "energy" more than voltage and current. The idea of S-parameters is to avoid the need to "perfectly" model an RF circuit or component with all the inherent subtleties, strays, and parasitics—which are often unknown and even unknowable—and then do a classic Spice-like analysis based on voltage, current, impedance, and frequency.

Not only would such a model and its associated analysis be complicated and time-consuming, but it would also not be accurate in simplifying the model versus reality. Instead, S-parameters view the component or circuit as a black box with unknown internal models that can be assessed and designed solely by the input-versus-output characteristics in multiple directions.

S-parameters are complex numbers (numbers with real and imaginary parts) that can be used directly or in a matrix to show reflection/transmission characteristics (amplitude and optionally phase) in the frequency domain. When a complex time-varying signal is passed through a linear network, the amplitude and phase shifts can dramatically distort the time-domain waveform. Therefore both amplitude and phase information in the frequency domain are important. S-parameters are the parameter that supports both information and has many advantages for high-frequency device characterization.

As with h-parameters, it begins with a two-port network. The output is not short- or open-circuited as it is with h-parameters (it is challenging to create a "perfect" short or open circuit at higher frequencies). Instead, it is terminated with the characteristic impedance of the component or circuit, usually but not always 50 Ω. (Note that most RF work is at 50 Ω, but for various reasons, cable TV and related technologies are usually at 75 Ω; why that is so is an interesting story for another time).

S-parameters and the resultant scattering matrix is an arrangement that quantifies how RF energy propagates through a multi-port network. It allows accurate characterization and description of the properties of components and circuits, including their many parasitic and stray values, as simpler "black boxes." This avoids the need to try to model the impedances, resistors, capacitances, and inductances of the circuit at the higher frequencies, where such modeling would be very difficult and likely miss many real-world subtleties.

There are four S-parameters for the two-port network: S11, S12, S22, and S21 (they are sometimes subscripted, sometimes not; there's a lot of inconsistency on this). The numbering convention for S-parameters is that the first number following the "s" is the port where the signal emerges, and the second number is the port where the signal is applied (Figure 2). For example, S21 is a measure of the signal coming out of port 2 relative to the RF stimulus entering port 1. When the numbers are the same (e.g., S11), it indicates a reflection measurement where the input and output ports are the same. S parameters can also be expressed in dB, as 20 log10 |Sxy| where x and y = 1 or 2.

Reflection parameters S11/S22 indicate reflection (return loss, often denoted by Greek upper-case tau τ), impedance, admittance, and VSWR. Transmission parameters S21/S12 show gain/loss (insertion loss), phase, and group delay (delay time).

4.10 Advantages of S-Parameters

The previous equations show one of the important advantages of s-parameters, namely that they are simply gains and reflection coefficients, both familiar quantities to engineers. By comparison, some of the y-parameters described earlier in this article are not so familiar. For example, the y-parameter corresponding to insertion gain s21 is the 'forward trans-admittance' y21 given by equation 3. Clearly, insertion gain gives by far the greater insight into the operation of the network.

Another advantage of s-parameters springs from the simple relationship between the variables a1, a2 , b1, and b 2, and various power waves:

$$|a_1|^2 = \text{Power incident on the input of the network.}$$
$$= \text{Power available from a source impedance } Z_0.$$

$$|a_2|^2 = \text{Power incident on the output of the network.}$$
$$= \text{Power reflected from the load.}$$

$$|b_1|^2 = \text{Power reflected from the input port of the network.}$$
$$= \text{Power available from a } Z_0 \text{ source minus the power}$$
$$\text{delivered to the input of the network.}$$

$$|b_2|^2 = \text{Power reflected from the output port of the network.}$$
$$= \text{Power incident on the load.}$$
$$= \text{Power that would be delivered to a } Z_0 \text{ load.}$$

The previous four equations show that s-parameters are
simply related to power gain and mismatch loss,
quantities which are often of more interest
than the corresponding voltage functions:

$$\left|s_{11}\right|^2 = \frac{\text{Power reflected from the network input}}{\text{Power incident on the network input}}$$

$$\left|s_{22}\right|^2 = \frac{\text{Power reflected from the network output}}{\text{Power incident on the network output}}$$

$$\left|s_{21}\right|^2 = \frac{\text{Power delivered to a } Z_0 \text{ load}}{\text{Power available from } Z_0 \text{ source}}$$

$$= \text{Transducer power gain with } Z_0 \text{ load and source}$$

$$\left|s_{12}\right|^2 = \text{Reverse transducer power gain with } Z_0 \text{ load and source}$$